MINI SULK

more sappy comics!

PUBLISHED BY TOP SHELF PRODUCTIONS
PO BOX 1282 MARIETTA GA 30061-1282 USA
TOP SHELF IS: CHRIS STAROS AND BRETT WARNOCK
TOP SHELF PRODUCTIONS ® AND TOPSHELF LOGO ARE REGISTERED TRADEMARKS OF TOP SHELF PRODUCTIONS INC.
COVER PRODUCTION BY PAUL HORNSCHEMEIER.
MANY THANKS ARE DUE TO FAMILY, FRIENDS, AND FANS, SO THANK YOU.

ISBN 189183066X

1ST PRINTING APRIL 2005. PRINTED IN CANADA.

MY BROTHER KNOWS KUNG FU

SURPRISE

snicke
HA HA!
SMACK
HEY! I'M BLEEDING
SORRY. YOU SHOULDN'T SURPRISE ME RIGHT AFTER KUNG FU CLASS.
MAYBE I'LL TELL MOM AND DAD..

BIRTHDAY GIFT

WHAT THE HELL? THIS ISN'T G.I. JOE.
OH... IT'S A BOOK.
WHAT'S IT FOR?
IT'S FOR MAKING LITTLE PAPER CONSTRUCTIONS.
DOUG PICKED IT OUT HIMSELF.
FLIP
FLIP
FLIP

YOU LIKE MAKING THINGS OUT OF CARDBOARD AND STUFF... YOU DO THAT KIND OF THING...
I DO?
WHAT'S NEXT?

SQVISH
DOUGLASSS!!
HEE HEE
HEEHEE
HA HA HA

TICKLE

LET'S TICKLE JEFF
NO STOP!
HA HA HA NO HA
HEE HEE
HA!
HA HA!
BRAPPPP!
HA HA
HEE HEE
HA HA
BRAP!
BRAP!
HA HA STOP!

LUNCHBOX

LOOK AT THE PUSSIES!
HAW!
WHAT'D YOU SAY?
SHOVE
HAHA
SHOVE
SMAK!
UH!
WUMP

ELBOW

HEE HEE HEE
HEE HEE
RRR
CLIK
CLIK
LET ME IN!!
HEE HA
HA HA
BANG
BANG
CRASH
OH SHIT!
KLIK
KLAK
HOLY SHIT!
GET SOME TOWELS!

NUNCHUCKS

CANADA

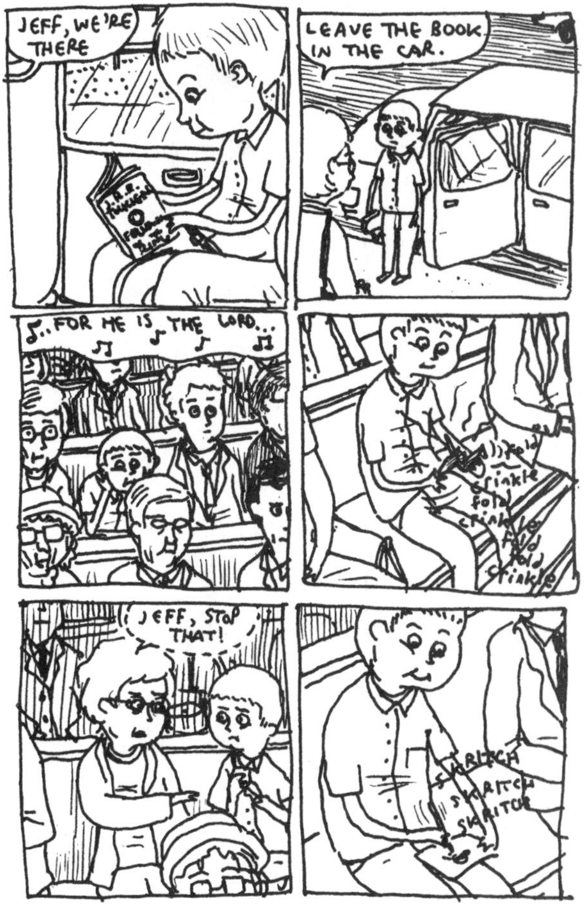

JEFF, WE'RE THERE
LEAVE THE BOOK IN THE CAR.
..FOR ME IS THE LORD...
fold
crinkle
fold
crinkle
fold
fold
crinkle
JEFF, STOP THAT!
SKRITCH
SKRITCH
SKRITCH

JEFF! GIVE ME THAT.
FIDGET
FIDGET
BONK
BONK
BONK
BONK
BONK
BONK
BONK
WHAT?
STOP!
BONK
BONK
BONK
BONK
BONK
BONK

JEFFREY DAVID BROWN!
FINALLY
YOU ARE IN BIG TROUBLE!
HEY!
WHUMP
DOUG'S THE ONE WHO PL--
THAT'S BECAUSE AN OLD WOMAN YELLED AT HIM FOR THE NOISE YOU WERE MAKING! YOU WERE VERY BAD!
WE'RE TAKING AWAY YOUR LORD OF THE RINGS BOOKS
I THINK WE SHOULD TAKE AWAY YOUR PRESENTS. YOU SHOULDNT EVEN GET A BIRTHDAY AT ALL

SPANK

YOU LITTLE BUGGER!
DOUGLAS!
I told you you'd get a spanking!
NO!
dodge
SMACK!
WHERE ARE MOM AND DAD GOING?
TO THE EMERGENCY ROOM.
I DON'T THINK DAD'S GOING TO SPANK US ANYMORE

WRASSLIN'

OKAY, OKAY, I GIVE!
YOU SHOULD WRESTLE DOUG NOW.
NO
I THOUGHT YOU'RE SUPPOSED TO BE THE GRAPPLING EXPERT. SCARED?
NO.
GIVE UP!
NO!
OKAY, I GIVE, I GIVE
YOU'RE TOO FAT
CLAP CLAP

NO HOLDS BARRED

REDWINGS

DID THEY WIN?
NO, IT'S IN OVERTIME
OOOH!
QUIET PLEASE
SORRY DAD
SCORE!
YAAAYYYY!
C'MON NOW!
WOO HOO!
YES!
WE WERENT DOING ANYTHING
THEN WHO THREW THIS SHIRT ON MY HEAD?!
HEE HEE

SNAP

WHAT ARE YOU GETTING?
UM, LEMON-HEADS, ALEXANDER THE GRAPES...
HEY STUPIDS!
FUCK YOU!
HAHA
HA HA HA
SNAP!
SNAP!
SNAP!
SNAP!
STOP!
LEAVE US ALONE!
SNAP!
SNAP!
SNAP!

WHERE'S MOM AND DAD?
WHAT'S WRONG?
THERE'S TWO GUYS ON BIKES TRYING TO FIGHT US OR SOMETHING
WHERE?
AT THE END OF THE STREET

WHY ARE YOU MESSING WITH MY FAMILY?
I WASN'T
THEN WHY DID MY BROTHER COME HOME CRYING?
DON'T EVER BOTHER MY FAMILY AGAIN
KOFF KOFF

NO ONE MUST KNOW

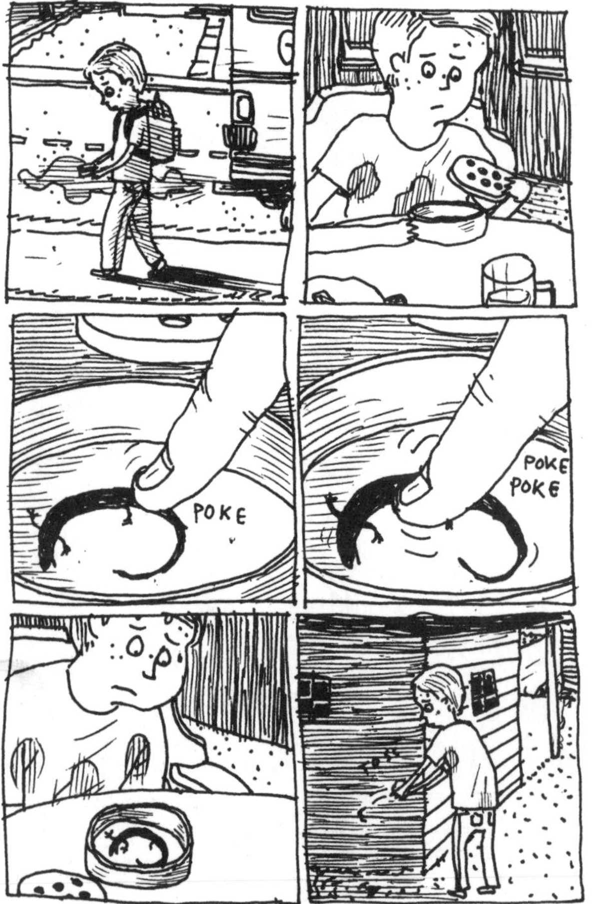
POKE
POKE
POKE

Yaaaay, Bite your Nails!

I'M USELESS

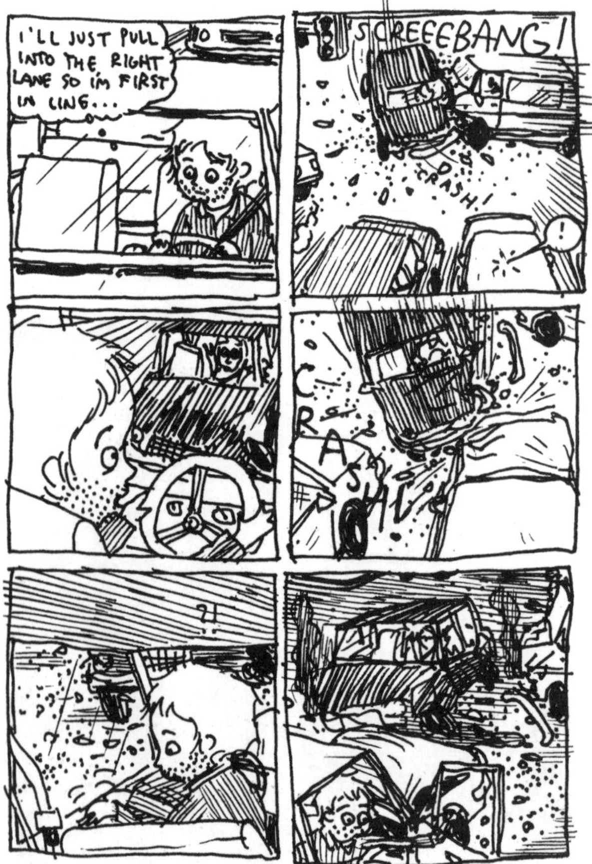
I'LL JUST PULL INTO THE RIGHT LANE SO I'M FIRST IN LINE...
SCREEEBANG!
CRASH!
!
CRASH!
?!

ARE YOU OKAY?
I DON'T KNOW
UM, WHAT'S YOUR NAME?
SOB
UH... DON'T WORRY HELP'S COMING, OKAY?
SOB

I NEED MORE COFFEE!

CUTE GIRLS ARE CUTE!

I like cheese

hat

HI JEFF
HI
I LIKE THE TOP OF YOUR HAT--
HEY!
FWAP
FWAP
OW
HOW'D YOU LIKE IT IF I HIT YOUR HEAD?
I WAS TRYING TO BE NICE TO YOU, JERK
WHY DON'T YOU TRY TO GO HOME, YOU STUPID JERK

recess

WOW. THE NEW GIRL IS SO CUTE. I THINK I LIKE HER
DON'T TELL SCOTT BUT I LIKE THE NEW GIRL
I LIKE THE NEW GIRL.
DON'T TELL BRIAN THAT, THOUGH

smurf

CAN YOU DRAW A SMURF?
YEAH
HA HA! THAT'S PERFECT! THANKS
THANKS JEFF. THAT WAS SWEET OF YOU.
HUH?
THE SMURF DRAWING YOU GAVE TO CHAS TO GIVE TO ME
HE GAVE YOU THAT? I DREW THAT BECAUSE HE ASKED ME TO...

poetry is sexy

girls are stupid

HI.
HI.
HOW WAS YOUR WEEKEND?
IT WAS OKAY.
MAN, I WAS A LOSER IN HIGH SCHOOL AND NOW THAT I'M MARRIED ALL THESE CUTE YOUNGER GIRLS ALL HANG ON ME..

thanks anyway

YOU DIDN'T HAVE TO BE SUCH A FUCKER

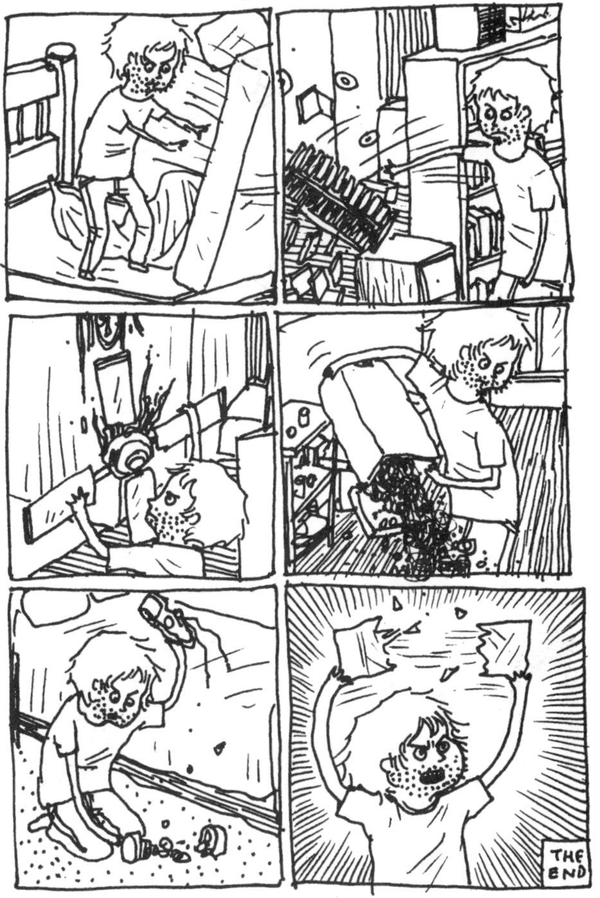
THE
END

HELP, I'M DROWNING!

SPLASH
SPLASH
SPLASH
HUH... SO THAT'S WHAT UNDERTOW FEELS LIKE
SPLASH
SPLASH
SPLASH
AH!
SPLASH
SPLASH
ACK! CAN'T-- BLEH --HELFPH!
DO YOU NEED SOME HELP JEFF?
SPLASH
ACK! COUGH! SPUTTER!
SPLASH
SPLASH
SPLASH
THANKS SEAN
SPLASH
SPLASH

ACTION TELEVISION SHOW!
METAL PIPE GANG!
WE DON'T NEED THESE GUNS! EXCEPT MAYBE, LIKE, OUR MAIN GUY!
YEAH! WE'LL JUST USE MARTIAL ARTS INSTEAD!
YEAH! BUT ISN'T MARTIAL ARTS REALLY ONLY SUPPOSED TO BE USED FOR DEFENSE?
YEAH! BUT WE AREN'T EVEN GOING TO REALLY LEARN IT. AFTER ALL, WE'VE GOT ALL THESE GREAT METAL PIPES!

AAAH!
HOLY SHIT!

OOF!

KRAK!

WOW! DID YOU SEE HER BREASTS? THEY WERE AMAZING!
WHERE'D ALL THESE EMPTY BARRELS COME FROM? WE DON'T EVEN NEED THESE..!

MY PATHETIC DAY

BITCH GET OFF THE PHONE

CRACK·THUD

the end

SNOW PARKING

THE NEXT DAY AFTER WORK
I SHOULD MOVE MY CAR... I'M JUST GONNA TAKE A QUICK NAP FIRST... ≷YAWN≶
SCRAAAAAAAAPE
HUH?
SHIT! HE'S PLOWING ME IN!
SCRAAAAAAAPE
FUCK! A TICKET!
WHY DIDN'T HE JUST COME OVER AND ASK ME TO MOVE MY CAR? LEAVE A NOTE? SHIT!

GOOD. YOU'RE MOVING YOUR CAR... I WAS GOING TO GIVE YOU A TICKET
YOU ALREADY GAVE ME A TICKET. I'M SORRY--
YOU THE OWNER OF THE PROPERTY?
YEAH
I'VE NEVER SEEN THAT CAR IN MY LIFE
I SAID I WAS SORRY
I LIVE ACROSS THE STREET! I'M PARKED OUT THERE EVERY DAY!
JUST MOVE YOUR CAR
I AM. I HAVE TO SHOVEL IT OUT
THAT'S GOOD ENOUGH. C'MON. NOW.
@#$?★!

misty

A KITTY!
WE RESCUED IT FROM A TREE IN THE CEMETARY
LET'S GIVE IT MILK
HEE HEE
CAN WE KEEP IT?
MEW
JEFF, YOU'RE ALLERGIC TO CATS

NO I'M NOT. THIS IS JUST HAY FEVER
PLEASE PLEASE PLEASE CAN WE KEEP IT? I'VE ALWAYS WANTED A KITTY OTHERWISE IT'LL BE COLD AND IT MIGHT GET HURT..
WELL, SHE CAN STAY TONIGHT. WE CAN PUT HER IN THE BACK ROOM IN THE BASEMENT
YAY!
GOOD NIGHT KITTY
THE NEXT DAY...
KITTY KITTY KITTY!
KITTY!
MEW

HEE HEE
AWWWWW
PURRRR RRRRR RRRR
PURRRRRRRRRRRRRRRRRR
PURRRRRRRRRRRRRRRRRRR
PURRRRRRRRRRRRRRRRRRRRR
KNEAD
KNEAD

MROWR?
AIEEE! DEVIL CAT!
MROWR PURRRR
MOM!
HM?
THE KITTY IS MEAN IT WAS GROWLING AT ME AND CLAWING AND BITING MY BATHROBE
JEFF, THAT'S JUST PURRING! IT MEANS THE KITTY IS HAPPY.
OH.

SHARE A CIGARETTE.

SHARE A MOMENT.

WHEN WILL MY SUPERPOWERS MANIFEST THEMSELVES?

MOST LIKELY SUPER POWER*:

SHOOTING ELECTRICTY OUT OF HANDS

(* SECOND MOST LIKELY: STEEL CLAWS GROWING OUT OF FOREARMS)

LATER...
LOOK!
THAT KID SAW US!
GET HIM!
NEVER!
AAUUGHH!
KAPOW!
WE THOUGHT WE WERE DEAD, BUT SUDDENLY THERE WAS A FLASH OF LIGHT..
IF ONLY I COULD TELL THEM IT WAS I WHO SAVED THEIR LIVES...

SOMEWHERE, OUT THERE

WE'LL HANG OUT, GO FOR WALKS, TALK FOR HOURS, FALL ASLEEP GAZING LOVINGLY INTO EACH OTHERS' EYES..
YEP, SHE'S OUT THERE, SOMEWHERE...
DAMMIT
WHERE IS SHE?

WHAT DID YOU THINK?

MORNING
KLANG
ROOMATE GETTING READY FOR WORK
C'MON, JASPER, LEAVE
YEAH
LEAVE SO WE CAN GO BACK TO SLEEP FOR AN HOUR
LEAVE SO WE CAN HAVE SEX THIS MORNING
SO
MM?
MMUM
UNH AH UH

Z
FLOP!
JEFFREY I HAVE TO GET READY FOR WORK
UNH
Z
I'M GOING TO WORK. YOU'LL BE BY LATER?
MMHm

FUCKING ARTISTS

MY MOST HATED ENEMY

THE SCIENTISTS

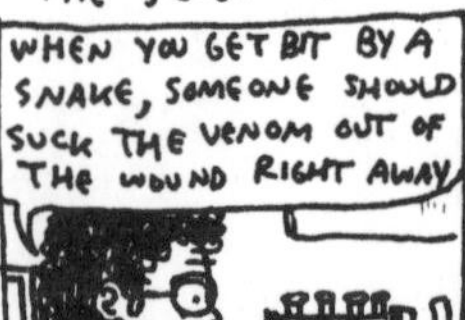

sensitive guy
OH DAMMIT! DID I LEAVE THE STOVE ON? WAIT... DID I? SHIT...

sensitive guy
OH, HOLD ON A SECOND, I WROTE YOU A POEM.

what're you doing?
I'm indulging my paranoid fantasies

YOU'RE NOT FAT... THAT'S JUST, LIKE, THE FORESHORTENING OF THE MIRROR AND STUFF...

I WANT TO BE THE FIRST ME

STOP "SOFTLY TOUCHING" ME

STOP CRYING!
WAHHH!
OR I'LL GIVE YOU SOMETHING TO REALLY CRY ABOUT!
WAHHH!
sniff
but I'm already crying.

I'M NOT KIDDING

TEST YOUR MIGHT

WHAT ARE YOU DOING?
SOMETIMES YOU HAVE TO DESTROY SOMETHING BEAUTIFUL TO MAKE SURE IT DOESN'T FALL INTO THE WRONG HANDS.

TO WENATCHEE

BY JEFFREY BROWN

REYHOUND
KLAK
KLAK
CAN WE GET THIS GUY A SEAT?
THIS GUY NEEDS A SEAT REAL BAD..

THANK YOU
I THINK I'VE GOT HIS NUMBER HERE...
BIP
BIP

YEAH... I'M STRANDED HERE IN A REAL BAD WAY SO...
IF YOU COULD GIVE ME A CALL, AH...
SO ARE YOU FROM SEATTLE?

WELL, I MOVED HERE FROM FLORIDA
I GOT IN OVER MY HEAD DOWN THERE
THEN I GOT THAT CLEARED UP AND I MOVED HERE TO GET BACK ON MY FEET
BUT THINGS DIDN'T PAN OUT REALLY..

AND NOW I DON'T...
WELL
YOU'VE GOT ONE FRIEND AND THAT'S JESUS CHRIST

THAT'S RIGHT
HE'LL NEVER LEAVE YOU TO SATAN, NEVER
NEVER

YOU'VE GOT THAT ALL FOLDED DIFFERENTLY?
YEP

SO YOU CAN TELL THE DIFFERENCE
YOU'RE SMART.
HERE. I HOPE THIS HELPS
OH, THANK YOU BROTHER

WELL, I HOPE THINGS WORK OUT FOR YOU
I'M SURE THEY WILL.

I'M HERE LEARNING TO BECOME SELF RELIANT

I'M TAKING CLASSES, SO I CAN, YOU KNOW, LEARN HOW TO COOK AND THINGS

HOW OLD ARE YOU?

I'M TWENTY ONE

YOU'RE JUST A YOUNG GUY
I USED TO BE PART OF THIS GROUP CALLED FAITH UNLIMITED...
WE'D GO TO PRISONS AND SING, MINISTER TO THE PRISONERS...

AND THAT...
THAT WAS THE LAST TIME I FELT CLOSE TO GOD...

SNIFF

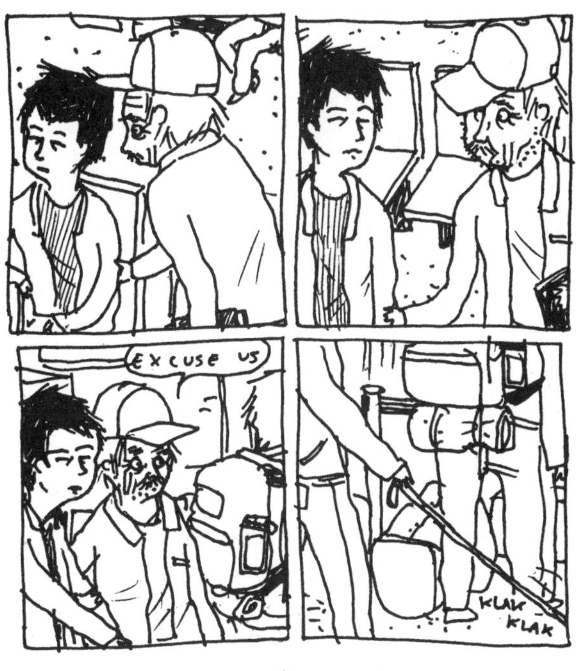
EXCUSE US
KLAK
KLAK

KLAK
KLAK
WHICH BUS IS THIS THE LINE FOR?
VANCOUVER.
THANKS
FIN

MUSEUM OF NATURAL HISTORY

Oh, what is it?

Give that back to me, Jesus, I need it
NO

GRAMPS

SO AS YOU CAN SEE HERE, IT TURNS OUT THAT FAILURE IS JUST ONE OF MANY OPTIONS...

GODDAM PARKING BRAKE

WE'RE STILL ADJUSTING TO EACH OTHER'S KISSING STYLES

THOSE BASTARDS

FOR MORE OF THE SAME, VISIT:

www.topshelfcomix.com

AND

www.theholyconsumption.com

ALSO EMAIL OR WRITE TO ME:

jeffreybrownrq@hotmail.com

PO BOX 120 DEERFIELD IL 60015